Advice to a Young Poet

Max Jacob

Advice to a Young Poet

Conseils à un jeune poète

Translated from French
and introduced by John Adlard

with a preface by Edmond Jabès
and an afterword by Jacques Evrard
translated by John Adlard

Shearsman Books & The Menard Press

Published in the United Kingdom in 2023 by
Shearsman Books   &   The Menard Press
PO Box 4239   8 The Oaks
Swindon   Woodside Avenue
SN3 9FN   London
                                        N12 8AR

Shearsman Books Ltd Registered Office
30–31 St. James Place, Mangotsfield, Bristol BS16 9JB
(this address not for correspondence)

www.shearsman.com

ISBN 978-1-84861-862-6

Original text first published by Éditions Gallimard, Paris, 1945.

This translation was first published by
The Menard Press, London, 1976.

*This book has been set in Le Monde Livre, with
section titles and poem titles in Requiem Fine.*

CONTENTS

Preface

Max Jacob: Man of the Secret

The last message I sent to Max Jacob, in February 1944, via the Apostolic Delegation in Cairo, where I lived – twenty-five words of affection and concern – was returned to me with a note on the back: *Deceased.*

> *What remains is the future,*
> *Not the present which breaks my heart.*

The future, for Max, is today; for thirty years it has been every day; for a long time yet it will be tomorrow; for his work holds us ceaselessly, and largely by just what eluded the best of his contemporaries: that is to say, by the seriousness of Play.

'The voices said to me *na*, which means *secret* in Hebrew,' he had written in the *Défense de Tartuffe*.

Man of the secret and not of a legend, Max Jacob, though careful of the legend, is intent on piercing the mystery of an existence dedicated to Heaven and Hell.

There is always a beyond – or a within – lived or to be lived, in the least significant sentences of his work. Poetry transfigures them. Poetry, that permanent mystery into which enter all mysteries.

Extremes, extravagances nourished by humour, disarming excesses controlled or uncontrolled are ridges enumerated on the horizon: no doubt difficult passages towards God; for God, who became the centre of his meditation from the famous night when Christ appeared to the poet, is also the pace which precedes the pace on his road.

Situating himself with regard to God and language, that was his constant care.

He writes for the benefit of Marcousis: 'We are inexpressible simple fellows and I wish *you* to express yourself by something ... which hardly expresses you, but with luck expresses something which isn't you but expresses something of you.' *[Rivage]*

In the possibility which is given us to speak dwells the impossibility of expressing ourselves.

To express with luck something which isn't oneself but expresses something of oneself, that is the aim of all creation The work is its revelation.

Haunted by suicide – had he not written, as early as 1919: 'Quarrels, the growth of insatiable pride, all intoxications do not silence the secret and obsessive idea of suicide'? – and as if he had constantly to redeem himself by destroying himself, he advanced towards the death reserved for him by the yellow star sewn on his jacket: a death glimpsed time and time again.

Edmond Jabès

INTRODUCTION

It was in June 1941, less than three years before his death in the Nazi camp at Drancy, that Max Jacob wrote *Advice to a Young Poet* in an exercise book bought at a grocer's, and presented it to Jacques Evrard of Montargis, a student of medicine, eighteen years old.[1] Marcel Béalu gave an account of this episode in his preface when he edited the text in 1945. Now, for the first time, as an afterword to this translation, the 'young poet' himself offers a different account.

In *Advice to a Young Poet* Max sets out to answer a question posed by the young man's father: 'What is a lyrical line?' It is his last major statement on poetry, the final development of the thinking of twenty-five years. 'Men used to believe,' he wrote in the 1916 preface to *Le Cornet à Dés*, 'that artists are inspired by angels and that there are different categories of angels.' By 1941, after the years of prayer and contemplation at Saint-Benoît-sur-Loire, this is no longer what 'men used to believe', but a fact in the interior life of a poet, the interior life without which a poet cannot be permeable. Only in a mind that is permeable is that conflagration possible ('the conflagration,' he called it in his *Art Poétique* of 1922,[2] 'after the encounter of a harmonious man with himself') which produces the lyrical line, the 'consecrated line' identified by its euphoria and its euphony. Permeability is a condition of both thought and feeling, yet poetry has nothing to do with ideas. However, ideas 'cease to be ideas if you feel them with passion, with experience, if you transform them into feelings.' This is almost the axiom in *Art Poétique*: 'One thinks well with ideas become forces of conviction or feeling.'[3] One must also describe with passion, and to do this one must study syntax, one must know every possibility of syntactic variation. In letters to

Jean Rousselot Max gave the same advice and praised the 'varied syntax' of Verlaine.[4]

The conflagration which produces the 'consecrated line' gives density, linguistic density, which is a sign of maturity, of major writing, of essential seriousness. Nineteen years before, in *Art Poétique*, he described that linguistic density as 'the principal charm of the 17th Century' and something no one cared much for today.[5] The vital paradox lies in the fact that, despite the primacy of seriousness, 'art is a game – so much the worse for anyone who makes a duty of it.' This is what the theologian Hugo Rahner urges us to understand. 'A true and full human being,' he writes, 'must be a creature of light-hearted, carefree play, a creature whose play is filled with the spirit and is, for that very reason, serious.'[6] And Max, too, tells his young poet to be a true human being, to be a Christian, to be a man, to be a poet-man, that is, a permeable man. The creator of sublime literature must be himself sublime. That does not mean sermons; the great comic writers are also sublime. 'Max had a great comic gift,' Picasso, in his old age, told his young mistress, recalling Montmartre days when Max and he were theatre-lovers ejected for eating sausages and Max could always make him laugh with monologues or with dialogues in which he took each part.[7]

In 1917 Max wrote to Jacques Doucet: 'You have already understood, dear sir, that I abhor naturalism, realism…'[8] Now, in 1941, he tells us to be realists, but qualifies this. We should be realists who are permeable. Unlike most realists he believes firmly in inspiration, in angels good and bad. He echoes St. John's warning: 'Beloved, believe not every spirit…' He also believes that the poet performs an act of magic, and he expects Jacques Evrard to believe so. The scope of that magic was clearly explained to Jacques Doucet twenty-four years before; it was what Max called the 'situation' of a work of art. 'I understand by situation,'

he wrote, 'that kind of magic which separates a work (even a pictorial or musical work) from the lover of art, that kind of transplantation which makes the work set your feet in another universe.' In *Art Poétique*, 1922, a situated work was 'a work surrounded by silence'.[10]

To believe in inspiration is not to strike a passive attitude; the poet must be like Rockefeller, intent on making a fortune from every object he touches. He should never read mediocrities. Yet in the nineteen-twenties Yvon Belaval found Max reading the verses of Joséphin Soulary, to 'set himself going', as Bach 'set himself going by playing the music of mediocre composers.'[11] A poet should never be bored, unless it is the positive boredom of a Byron, which is fertile ground. As long ago as 1922, in his little *Art Poétique*, he was considering different kinds of boredom.[12]

'Love a word,' he tells Jacques Evrard. 'Repeat it. Gargle with it.' Seventeen years before, in a letter to Jean Grenier, he recommended 'verbal sensuality.'[13] 'You must read the dictionary,' he told Belaval in 1927. 'Each day I read Larousse. How many astonishing words that we don't know or that we forget. You take a word, you break it, you turn it over, you turn it over again.'[14] Now he tells Jacques Evrard that round a word a line, a strophe coagulate. That is exteriorisation. He insists (as he did in that letter to Jean Grenier in 1924) that poetry must be concrete. 'The abstract is bad and boring.' He told Grenier 'not to be afraid of the word which strikes, which colours, which, above all, makes concrete, which synthesises.'[15] 'Avoid clichés,' he urged Armand and Lucienne Salacrou in the same year.[16] Now, in 1941, he recognises that, although the poet is not a man of clichés, he must use some for fear of being incomprehensible.

He tells Jacques Evrard: 'Exteriorising is everything.' Yet he admits that each has his own method; the point of departure may be erudition, the observation of human life, or a single word repeated with love. But how few

works are really exteriorised! 'With Balzac it's always Balzac speaking.' But Musset in his comedies exteriorises, and so does Shakespeare.

On style Max quotes the rather hackneyed words of Buffon: 'Style is the man' – as he quoted them in 1916, in the preface to *Le Cornet à dés*. Then he commented that this meant a writer must write with his blood, adding that the definition seemed to him 'salutary' but 'not exact.' Style was 'the will to exteriorise oneself by chosen means.' But in 1941 he seems more satisfied with Buffon's axiom, explaining it as meaning' 'what is most profound in the breast and blood of man.' In 1916 he was anxious to distinguish style from situation; now it is development that he stresses. 'Develop,' he says. 'All art, of whatever kind, is in that word.' And as a preliminary exercise one should write plenty of pastiches, in order not to write them unintentionally, This was an exercise which always pleased Max. Yvon Belaval remembered him improvising Hugoesque verses with great gusto more than a decade earlier.[17]

Max has little enthusiasm for youthful success; it is mostly an embarrassment in later years. There is no need to be in a hurry, no need to catch the spirit of the age before it fades, anything worth saying being eternal and the spirit of the age mere fashion. 'Abhor fashion,' Max told the Salacrous in 1925. 'Love only that fashion you create."[18] Hard work is the first requirement and there are three conditions of work: separation, silence and ignorance – by which last he implies astonishment, which means candour, and 'candour is the road to all discoveries in art as in science.' And part of that hard work is the taking of notes. Otherwise the loss is incalculable. Yvon Belaval received the same advice when he left for America in 1930.[19] So much for work – the essential gift, he wrote to Marcel Béalu a few months before *Advice to a Young Poet*, is 'the gift of love and sorrow.'[20] This was not a passing thought; it is repeated in verse:

On the walls of Edinburgh
So much sorrow
Is espoused to so much love
That your courser Poetry
Wears a veil of black tonight.[21]

JOHN ADLARD

Notes

[1] In his Gallimard edition, Marcel Béalu always refers to the
'young poet' as 'J.E.' Among others, René Plantier (*Max
Jacob*, Paris, 1972, p. 11) has stated that *Conseils à un jeune
poète* was written 'for the poet, Edmond Jabès', Even
before we learned the identity of 'J.E.' from Marcel Béalu,
Edmond Jabès informed us that M. Plantier's statement
was not correct. Jacques Evrard is now [1976] a surgeon.

[2] P. 26.

[3] P. 11.

[4] Jean Rousselot: *Max Jacob: L'homme qui faisait penser à Dieu*,
Paris, 1946, pp. 113, 119.

[5] P. 28.

[6] Hugo Rahner: *Man at Play*, translated by Brian Battershaw
and Edward Quinn, London, 1965, pp. 3, 4.

[7] Genevieve Laporte: *Sunshine at Midnight*, translated by Doug-
las Cooper, London, 1975, pp. 5, 6.

[8] François Garnier, editor; Max Jacob, *Correspondance*, Volume I,
Paris, 1953, p. 133.

[9] Garnier, p. 132.

[10] P. 28.

[11] Yvon Belaval: *La Rencontre avec Max Jacob*, Paris, 1946, page 29.

[12] Pp. 19, 20.

[13] Max Jacob: *Lettres à un ami. Correspondance, 1922–1933*, avec
Jean Grenier, Lausanne, 1951, p. 41.

[14] Belaval, p. 27.

[15] *Lettres à un ami*, p. 41.
[16] Max Jacob: *Lettres aux Salacrou*, 1923–1926, Paris, 1957, p. 65.
[17] Belaval, p. 29.
[18] *Lettres aux Salacrou*, p. 109.
[19] Belaval, pages 32, 33.
[20] Max Jacob: *Lettres à Marcel Béalu*, Lyon, 1959, p. 211.
[21] 'Angoisses et autres.'

CONSEILS
À UN JEUNE POÈTE

ADVICE
TO A YOUNG POET

J'ouvrirai une école de vie intérieure, et j'écrirai sur la porte: école d'art.

*

La vie intérieure est le discernement des esprits extérieurs, les discussions de la Raison avec ceux-ci. Les anges sont inégalement qualifiables, or que dire des démons? *Mais la voix de Dieu n'est pas celle de la Poésie.* Les génies ne sont pas Dieu bien qu'ils aient été créés par Lui. Apprenez donc à discerner ces voix inspiratrices et faites qu'en vous Dieu les domine. D'abord exercez-vous à Dieu, car c'est le meilleur fond de tableau, l'unique fond de tableau. Trouvez Dieu d'abord.

*

Le résultat premier de la vie intérieure est le nous rendre *perméable.* Un poète imperméable ne fera que des œuvres superficielles.

*

On peut se demander si toute poésie n'est pas autre chose que superficialité.

Je réponds «oui». C'est dommage. Mais on peut se demander à soi-même d'essayer autre chose. En tout cas ne vivront que les œuvres non superficielles, je veux dire celles qui, ayant l'apparence du superficiel, ont *passé par le gouffre du sérieux.*

Donc soyez d'abord *perméable,* c'est-à-dire sérieux.

*

I shall open a school of interior life and I shall write on the door *Art School.*

*

Interior life is distinguishing between exterior spirits, is Reason's discussions with them. Angels are not to be ranked equally, so what can you say of devils? *But the voice of God is not the voice of Poetry.* Geniuses are not God although they have been created by Him. Learn then to distinguish between these voices of inspiration and see that in you God controls them. First pray to God, the best background, the only background. Find God first.

*

The first result of interior life is to make us *permeable.* An impermeable poet will produce only superficial works.

*

It may be wondered whether all poetry is nothing but superficiality.

My reply is 'Yes'. It's a pity. But one can ask oneself to try something else. In any case only those works will live which are not superficial, I mean those which, for all their appearance of superficiality, have *passed through the abyss of the serious.*

First of all, then, be *permeable,* that is to say, serious.

*

L'invention!

Ce qui sauve l'art c'est l'invention. Il n'y a création que là où il y a invention. Chaque art a ses inventions. L'idée d'un bémol ou d'un dièze à l'endroit où on ne l'attendait pas est une invention. Une image nouvelle (oh que c'est rare!) peut-être une invention. Une couleur imprévue mise en sa place. Une proportion nouvelle dans la dimension d'une œuvre.

Mais la véritable invention vient d'une conflagration de pensées ou de sentiments.

*

Un vers lyrique est le résultat d'une conflagration. Seule la conflagration lui donne de la densité.

*

Réfléchissez à la question de la densité. Avez-vous constaté la différence entre l'eau de mer et l'eau de fontaine? Que votre vers et votre prose aient de la densité.

*

Presque toute la différence entre les grands et les petits auteurs est dans la densité de leur Verbe (et, bien entendu, dans le sérieux).

*

Maturité.

Une œuvre mûrie devient sérieuse. Une œuvre mûrie trouve d'elle-même son commencement, son milieu et sa fin. Un style mûri prend sa densité comme l'œuf prend de la consistance sous la poule. Un mot doit être aussi mûri qu'une œuvre entière: surtout l'épithète.

*

Invention!

What saves art is invention. There is creation only where there is invention. Each art has its own inventions. The idea of a flat or a sharp at a place where it was not looked for is an invention. A new image (how rare that is!) can be an invention. An unexpected colour put in its place. A new proportion in the dimension of a work.

But real invention comes from a conflagration of thoughts or feelings.

*

A lyrical line is the result of a conflagration. Only conflagration gives it density.

*

Ponder the question of density. Have you ascertained the difference between sea-water and spring-water? Let your verse and your prose have density.

*

Almost the whole difference between great and small authors lies in the density of their Word (and, it goes without saying, in their seriousness).

*

Maturity.

Maturing, a work becomes serious. A mature work finds its own beginning, middle and end. A mature style takes its density as the egg takes consistency under the hen. A word must be as mature as a complete work: the epithet above all.

*

Mais, direz-vous, vous me faites perdre la légèreté, l'élan, l'enthousiasme?

Pas du tout. Je vous enseigne la légèreté, l'élan, l'enthousiasme, car plus la source du jet d'eau est comprimée, plus il monte haut.

*

J'appelle maturité d'une œuvre sa descente aux enfers. Le Seigneur est descendu aux enfers avant l'Ascension.

*

Vous me direz: médecin, guéris-toi toi-même. Évidemment. Mais si je n'ai pas su profiter de mon esthétique, ce n'est pas une raison pour en fermer la porte aux autres.

*

L'originalité vraie ne peut être que dans la maturation, car ce qui est original c'est le fond de mon moi: le reste vient des autres et ne peut donc pas être original. Or ce qui est original plaît et non ce qui est déjà vu.

*

Ici pourrait se placer la question si grave des clichés. Le cliché est un mot de passe commode en conversation pour se passer de sentir. Un poète doit sentir tous ses mots, mais le bourgeois n'a pas le temps, de là des ponts commodes qu'on appelle «clichés». Le poète dose ses clichés: il ne peut y renoncer que sous peine d'être incompréhensible, à lui de savoir quand il peut placer le mot qui n'est pas une formule toute faite, de façon à être nouveau sans être obscur.

*

But, you will say, you are making me lose nimbleness, elan, enthusiasm?

By no means. I am teaching you nimbleness, elan, enthusiasm, for the more the fountain-head is compressed the higher the fountain soars.

*

I call the maturity of a work its descent into Hell. Our Lord descended into Hell before the Ascension.

*

You will tell me, 'Physician, heal thyself.' Of course. But if I have not been able to benefit from my aesthetics, that is no reason for shutting the door on others.

*

Real originality can only be in maturation, for what is original is the essence of my self; the rest comes from others and consequently can't be original. Now, what is original pleases and not what has been seen before.

*

Here a place might be found for the serious question of cliches. The cliché is a convenient password in conversation when you want to do without feeling. A poet must feel all his words, but the bourgeois hasn't time, hence the convenient bridges we call 'clichés'. The poet puts in the right proportion of clichés: he can't give them up for fear of being incomprehensible. It's for him to know when he can place the word which is not a ready-made formula, so as to be new without being obscure.

*

Cependant le vers est sacré s'il est le résultat d'une conflagration. Alors il ne faut pas avoir peur de l'incompréhensible. Le tact est de savoir si le vers est sacré ou non. Le vers sacré est conservé à cause de sa musique belle et non macaronique (cherchez des vers sacrés dans l'œuvre d'Apollinaire: il y en a quelques-uns). Le vers sacré est de belle venue, musical, euphonique, euphorique, luisant, et tel que le plus malheureux paysan dit en l'entendant: «Ah! que c'est beau!» et non pas: «qu'est-ce que ça veut dire»?

*

Le «qu'est-ce que ça veut dire?» est le reproche qu'on fait au poète qui n'a pas su vous émouvoir. Reproche grave entre tous.

*

Rendez-vous perméable, car comment obtiendrez-vous la conflagration lyrique si vous n'avez rien senti ni rien pensé.

*

«Ni rien pensé»? cela est discutable. Les idées n'ont rien à voir avec la poésie: *c'est l'inexprimable qui compte.* Les idées n'appartiennent pas à l'homme; elles viennent du ciel des images; on se les approprie. Rien de plus triste, de plus pesant que les idées; elles sont toutes de M. Prudhomme et de M. Homais. Elles cessent d'être des idées si vous les ressentez à mort, si vous les ressentez avec passion, avec expérience, si vous *les transformez en sentiments.*

*

However, the line is consecrated if it is the result of a conflagration. Then there's no need to be afraid of the incomprehensible. The tact lies in knowing whether the line is consecrated or not. The consecrated line is preserved because its music is beautiful and not macaronic (look for consecrated lines in the work of Apollinaire: there are a few). The consecrated line is finely grown, musical, euphonic, euphoric, shining, so that the most wretched peasant says, on hearing it, 'Oh, how beautiful!' and not, 'What does that mean?'

*

'What does that mean?' is the reproach you make to the poet who has failed to move you. A serious reproach in any company.

*

Make yourself permeable, for how will you obtain the lyrical conflagration if you have felt nothing and thought nothing?

*

'Thought nothing?' That's debatable. Ideas have nothing to do with poetry: *it's the inexpressible that counts.* Ideas don't belong to man; they come from the heaven of images; one adapts them to oneself. Nothing sadder, nothing heavier than ideas; they all belong to M. Prudhomme[1] and M. Homais.[2] They cease to be ideas if you feel them to the quick, if you feel them with passion, with experience, *if you transform them into feelings.*

*

Cela est la signification du culte si méconnu du Sacré-Cœur. La lance qui a traversé la poitrine de N.-S. J.-C. est la flèche indicatrice du chemin que prennent les idées pour devenir valables.

D'autre part, le Sang et l'eau sortis du Cœur sont l'image de l'union de l'Esprit avec la matière qui est la seule *compréhension* valable.

Je pense que vous me comprenez. *Faites descendre.*

*

Style descriptif = style scientifique. Le contraire même de la poésie. Byron disait: La poésie a horreur du raisonnement. Il aurait pu dire: et de la description scientifique. Si vous voulez décrire, décrivez avec passion et dans le style poétique.

*

Je n'entends pas par style le bric-à-brac des «azurs des anges, des ombrages», etc... mais j'entends la collaboration du sentiment.

*

Pour éviter le style description scientifique, variez avec soin votre syntaxe d'une phrase à l'autre. Je faisais jadis collection de formules syntaxiques: on n'en a jamais assez à sa disposition. La richesse du style est là; son naturel est là; son intérêt, son amusement est là.

*

Quand vous aurez une belle collection de syntaxes, ayez aussi tous les mots usuels, et si vous connaissez bien la grammaire vous serez un bon écrivain. Ce sera beaucoup, car il y a peu d'écrivains qui écrivent.

*

That is the meaning of the worship, so misjudged, of the Sacred Heart. The shaft which passed through the breast of Our Lord Jesus Christ is the arrow pointing the way ideas take to become valid.

On the other hand the Blood and water that issued from the Heart are the image of the union of the Spirit with matter, which is the only understanding that is valid.

I think you understand me. *Make it descend.*

*

Descriptive style = scientific style. The very opposite of poetry. Byron said, 'Poetry abhors reasoning.' He could have added, 'and scientific description.' If you want to describe, describe with passion and in poetic style.

*

To me style is not the odds and ends of 'azures, angels, shady nooks' etc., but the collaboration of feeling.

*

To avoid the style of scientific description vary your syntax carefully from one sentence to another. I used to collect syntactic formulas: you can never have enough at your disposal. There is to be found richness of style, there is its naturalness; its interest, its amusement are there.

*

When you have a fine collection of syntaxes, have all the usual words, too, and if you know grammar well you will be a good writer. That will be a great deal, for there are few writers who *write*.

*

Ce qui est écrit dure.

*

Ce qui n'est pas écrit dure, si cela apporte de la nouveauté, de la perméabilité (c'est synonyme), de l'invention.

*

Il ne faut pas «écrire» dans le marbre toute œuvre mais seulement ce qui en vaut la peine. Autrement on est risible. Exemple: «Je vais déjeuner», mais je ne dirai pas: «Je vais pourvoir ma chair et mon sang des aliments extérieurs qui les renouvellent.» Ce serait d'un effet comique certain. J'ai connu un monsieur qui parlait sur ce ton. Faites-moi penser à vous en parler.

Style poétique! C'est un style où les voyelles ont leur nombre, où les diphtongues sont pesées, où les consonnes se répètent ou ne se répètent pas. La propriété des termes y a moins d'importance que leur euphonie.

*

En poésie la valeur précise du mot n'a de valeur que si cette précision est exagérée. Corbière est plus qu'écrivain, il est poète quand ayant à définir des marins, il les appelle: «Ces anges mal léchés».

Cela est la poésie: c'est le bon style du poète.

Vous avez le choix entre ce style poétique parce que trop fort ou uniquement musical:

> Voie lactée, ô sœur lumineuse
> des blancs ruisseaux de Chanaan.

*

What is written lasts.

*

What is not written lasts if it brings novelty, permeability (it's synonymous), invention.

*

It's not necessary to 'write' every work in marble, but only what's worth the trouble. Otherwise you are ridiculous. For example: 'I'm going to have lunch' – but I shan't say, 'I'm going to provide my flesh and my blood with the exterior nutriments which renew them.' That would certainly have a comic effect. I knew a gentleman who talked like that. Remind me to tell you about him.

Poetic style! It's a style where vowels are well balanced, where diphthongs are weighed, where consonants are repeated or not repeated. There the propriety of terms has less importance than their euphony.

*

In poetry the precise value of the word has value only if this precision is exaggerated. Corbière is more than a writer, he is a poet when, having to define sailors, he calls them 'these ill-polished angels'.

That is poetry: it's the good style of the poet.

You have the choice between this style poetic because too strong or only musical.

> O Milky Way, O sister bright
> of the white brooks of Canaan.

*

Au fait, tout cela est inutile. La grande affaire est de vivre, vivre par l'imagination et la poitrine, d'inventer, de savoir, de jouer. L'art est un jeu.

Tant pis pour celui qui s'en fait un devoir.

*

Si vous n'êtes pas blessé par l'extérieur ou réjoui par l'extérieur, jusqu'à la souffrance, vous n'avez pas la vie intérieure et si vous n'avez pas la vie intérieure, votre poésie est vaine.

*

Il faut «encaisser» longuement et retarder la réaction. Plus on la retarde mieux ça vaut. Le «rendu» immédiat ne vaut rien, mais c'est l'élaboration de la transformation qui édifie et crée.

*

Demandez à un professeur de chant ce que c'est que placer sa voix.

Placez la vôtre au ventre comme un tambour. Ce qui ne vient pas du tambour n'est qu'enfantillage.

*

Concrétiser! Penser à ce mot. L'abstrait est mauvais et ennuyeux. Ayez un style concret où il soit question de choses, d'objets, de gens. Qui fait l'ange fait la bête, dit Pascal et il sort de la poitrine de Dieu de l'eau avec le Sang Esprit. L'eau est matière.

Très important: Concrétisez!

Concrétiser, ça ne veut pas dire la poésie populiste, les paysans, les sabots, etc., ça veut dire: placer votre voix dans le ventre, la pensée dans le ventre, et parler du sublime avec la voix dans le ventre.

In fact all that is useless. The great thing is to live, live by imagination and the heart, to invent, to know, to play. Art is a game.

So much the worse for anyone who makes a duty of it.

*

If you are not wounded by the exterior or gladdened by the exterior until it hurts, you have no interior life, and if you have no interior life your poetry is vain.

*

You must 'suffer in silence' for a long time and delay the reaction. The more it's delayed, the more it's worth. Immediate 'tit for tat' is worth nothing, but it is the working out of the transformation which edifies and creates.

*

Ask a singing teacher what is meant by placing one's voice.

Place yours in the belly like a drum. What doesn't come from the drum is only childishness.

*

Make it concrete! Ponder that word. The abstract is bad and boring. Have a concrete style dealing with things, objects, people. 'He who plays the angel plays the beast,' says Pascal, and from the breast of God water issues with the Blood of the Spirit. The water is matter.

Very important: Make it concrete!

Making concrete doesn't mean populist poetry, peasants, clogs etc., it means placing your voice in your belly, your thought in your belly, and speaking of the sublime with your voice in your belly.

*

Être réaliste, ça ne veut pas dire ne parler que des ouvriers et des bourgeois, ça veut dire: avoir l'esprit médical même en parlant des rois. Soyez réaliste et cultivez cette tendance qui est déjà en vous.

Réaliste tout en étant perméable.

*

Apollinaire avait horreur des «pièces d'anthologie», c'est-à-dire de la poésie parfaite. Il avait raison, je crois. Cependant, il faut aussi savoir faire cela à cause du respect pour l'art, et puis il en reste toujours quelque chose et suffisamment.

Étudiez donc la grammaire, la rhétorique, la métrique, la phonétique surtout.

Et oubliez le tout.

*

L'inspiration!

Si je crois à l'inspiration? Mais bien sûr! Je crois même que tous les hommes sont inspirés. Ça s'appelle intuition. Ça s'appelle tentation. Ça dépend de la personne qui inspire. On est inspiré par les anges, les démons et il y a toutes sortes d'anges et de démons. Mais il y a des génies parmi les anges. Quand on a un génie inspirateur, les critiques disent: «Il a du génie.» L'échelle de Jacob dans la Bible s'appuie sur Dieu: les anges vont et viennent tout du long. Les anges sont des émanations planétaires pas plus malins que des hommes; il faut donc discuter, en s'appuyant sur Dieu, leurs pauvres inspirations. Il y a des anges remarquables aussi; il faut les mériter, ou bien les recevoir de la bonté de Dieu. Il y a des démons inspirateurs de vols, de crimes, d'entêtement. Il faut prier Dieu de vous en débarrasser.

*

Being a realist doesn't mean speaking only of working men and middle-class people, it means speaking even of kings in the spirit of a doctor. Be a realist and cultivate that tendency which is already in you.

A realist, but a realist who is permeable.

*

Apollinaire abhorred 'anthology pieces', that is to say, perfect poetry. I think he was right. However, because of respect for art one must also be able to do that sort of thing, and then something always remains to make it worthwhile.

So study grammar, rhetoric, metrics, and above all phonetics.

And forget the lot.

*

Inspiration!

Do I believe in inspiration? Of course I do! I even believe that all men are inspired. It's called intuition. It's called temptation. It depends on the person who inspires. We are inspired by angels, by devils, and there are all kinds of angels and devils. But there are geniuses among the angels. When one is inspired by a genius, the critics say, 'He has genius.' Jacob's Ladder in the Bible leans on God: the angels come and go the whole length of it. Angels are planetary emanations no more mischievous than men; so, leaning on God, one has to discuss their poor inspirations. There are notable angels, too; these have to be deserved, or else received through the goodness of God. There are devils who inspire thefts, crimes, pig-headedness. One has to pray to God to be rid of them.

Donc l'inspiration doit être surveillée.

Examinez-vous. Cela s'appelle réflexion, double réflexion, se voir vivre, voir vivre les autres.

C'est la vie intérieure.

*

Ce qui fait un grand médecin ou un grand poète ce n'est pas le nombre de livres qu'ils ont lus, mais la qualité de leur vie intérieure: la digestion des connaissances et l'enquête.

*

On demandait à Rockefeller comment il avait fait fortune: «En cherchant comment on peut faire fortune avec chacun des objets que je touchais.» Idem pour la poésie, la littérature.

*

«C'est beau comme littérature», disait Jarry. Il y a une beauté littéraire. La chercher, la sentir, la créer, l'inventer.

*

N'écoutez pas le mal qu'on vous dira de moi de telle façon (en l'écoutant) que vous n'écoutiez pas mes maximes. Je peux n'avoir pas su ouvrir les portes que je vous désigne. C'est possible. Mais ces portes existent en dehors de moi et de vous. A vous de les ouvrir mieux que je n'ai fait.

*

Croyez bien que la bouche parle de l'abondance du cœur. Si vous êtes un beau cœur et un beau cerveau vous créerez de la beauté. Sinon vous créerez de la laideur,

So a watch must be kept on inspiration.

Examine yourself. That is called reflection, double reflection, seeing oneself living, seeing others living.

That is interior life.

*

What makes a great doctor or a great poet isn't the number of books he has read, but the quality of his interior life: the digestion of learning, and *enquiry.*

*

Rockefeller was asked how he had made his fortune. 'By looking to see how a fortune could be made out of every object that I touched.' The same for poetry, literature.

*

'As literature it's fine,' said Jarry. There is a literary beauty. Seek it out, feel it, create it, invent it.

*

Don't listen to the evil which people will tell you of me so that (listening to it) you won't listen to my maxims. I may not have been able to open the doors I point out to you. It's possible. But those doors exist outside me and outside you. It's up to you to open them better than I have.

*

Believe firmly that the mouth speaks from the abundance of the heart. If you are a heart of beauty and a brain of beauty, you will create beauty. Otherwise you will create

car le démon ne crée pas de la beauté. Les créateurs de sublime étaient sublimes dans leur vie. La bassesse de la littérature du xxe siècle vient de ce que c'est une époque basse, calculatrice, l'inventeuse du système D et autres ignominies.

*

Est-ce que ça veut dire d'écrire des sermons? Mais non! Regardez Rabelais! Grand initié qui vaut bien Platon! On peut être un auteur comique et être une âme de première qualité.

Soyez une âme de première qualité. Soyez chrétien, fréquentez les sacrements, confessez-vous, examinez-vous. Le xviie siècle était chrétien. Voltaire croyait en Dieu. Renan aussi. Picasso me disait: «Pense à Dieu et travaille.» L'examen de conscience quotidien est l'A.B.C. de la littérature. Pasteur et Branly communiaient tous les matins.

Si on vous dit le contraire, jugez d'abord la valeur de celui qui vous parle; c'est rarement quelqu'un de remarquable.

*

Faites une méditation quotidienne en vous levant, vous me direz des nouvelles de ce sport. Ce n'est pas du temps perdu mais c'est du temps gagné. Celui qui vous dira le contraire est un imbécile et je sais pourquoi. Peu à peu, vous étendrez la méditation à la médecine et à la poésie et vous deviendrez un homme, *ce qui est la première condition pour devenir un grand homme.*

*

Les gens s'imaginent que pour être poète il faut aligner des lignes inégales avec un demi-calembour au bout. Or pour être poète il faut être un homme d'abord, puis

ugliness, for the Devil doesn't create beauty. Creators of the sublime were sublime in their lives. The vileness of the literature of the 20th Century comes from the fact that it is a vile, calculating age which has invented the makeshift and other ignominies.

*

Does that mean writing sermons? No! Look at Rabelais! A great initiate, quite as great as Plato! You can be a comic author and a soul of the first order.

Be a soul of the first order. Be a Christian, go to the sacraments, go to confession, examine yourself. The 17th Century was Christian. Voltaire believed in God, so did Renan. Picasso used to say to me, 'Think of God and work.' Daily examination of conscience is the A.B.C. of literature. Pasteur and Branly went to Communion every morning.

If anyone tells you the opposite, first judge the speaker's worth; it's rarely anyone of note.

*

Make a daily meditation as you get up; this pastime will delight you. It's not time wasted but time gained. Anyone who tells you the opposite is an idiot and I know why. Little by little you will extend meditation to medicine and poetry and you will become a man, *which is the first condition for becoming a great man.*

*

People imagine that to be a poet you have to line up unequal lines with a half-pun at the end. Now, to be a poet you have to be, first of all, a man, then a Man-Poet.

un Homme-Poète. Autrement on est un petit oiseau beaucoup plus ridicule qu'un cochon. Les assemblées de petits jeunes gens à prétentions poétiques sont comiques, mais quelle beauté que la réunion d'hommes intelligents qui s'entretiennent de la Beauté comme les apôtres après la Résurrection s'entretenaient de leur ami Jésus-Christ.

*

Apollinaire était un homme costaud, puissant et beau. Rimbaud partant faire l'explorateur en Abyssinie a prouvé qu'il était un homme. Verlaine, au dire de son ami intime Paul Fort, *était un cuirassier.* Soyez un homme, c'est-à-dire une énergie, un buisson de sentiments, un caractère délimité. Soyez un homme perméable et non pas entêté.

Condition de la Beauté: qu'elle soit en vous.

*

L'érudition est bien loin d'être un mal; elle agrandit le champ de l'expérience et l'expérience des hommes et des choses est la base du talent. Ce n'est pas avec des livres qu'on fait des œuvres, bien sûr, mais dans les livres il est question des hommes et des choses et cela se confronte. D'ailleurs l'érudition c'est la mémoire et la mémoire, c'est l'imagination.

*

Tout se ramène à un vocabulaire et à une collection de formes syntaxiques? Non, certes, non.

Michel Manoll, seul grand critique que je connaisse, disait en parlant du poète Louis Émié, de Bordeaux: «Il a beaucoup d'humanité; il a beaucoup d'amour des mots, mais l'un ne rejoint pas l'autre.» Ou une phrase telle. Il disait: «Ce qui me frappe d'abord, c'est l'encre.»

Otherwise you're a wee birdie much more absurd than a pig. The meetings of little lads with poetic pretensions are comic, but what beauty there is in the gathering of intelligent men who hold converse with Beauty as the apostles after the Resurrection held converse with their friend Jesus Christ.

*

Apollinaire was a hefty man, powerful and good-looking. Rimbaud leaving to be an explorer in Abyssinia proved he was a man. Verlaine, in the words of his close friend Paul Fort, *was a guardsman.* Be a man, that is to say, an energy, a bush of feelings, a distinct character. Be a permeable man and not pig-headed.

Condition for Beauty: that it should be within you.

*

Learning is far from being a bad thing; it enlarges the field of experience, and the experience of men and of things is the basis of talent. Granted that it's not with books that one creates works, but books are about men and things and there is a comparison. Besides, learning is memory and memory is imagination.

*

Everything comes back to a vocabulary and a collection of syntactic forms? No, of course not.

Michel Manoll, the only great critic I know, had this to say about the poet Louis Émié of Bordeaux: 'He has a lot of humanity, he has a lot of love for words, but the one isn't linked with the other.' Or some such sentence. He would say, 'What strikes me first is ink.'

C'est cette jonction qui est tout. On peut faire des exercices brillants et aussi être un homme perméable et douloureux, mais si les exercices n'expriment pas l'homme perméable, on reste double et sans intérêt. On dit alors: il n'est pas sincère, mot qui ne veut pas dire grand'chose dans la bouche des sots mais qui veut dire beaucoup dans celle d'un connaisseur.

*

Ne vous ennuyez pas. L'ennui est un péché mortel en matière de poésie. L'ennui est l'enfer de la poésie… à moins d'un bel ennui, celui de Byron qui avait fait le tour des sciences, du monde, de la terre, des langues et de l'amour.

Mais cet ennui est si rare qu'il vaut mieux n'en pas parler (sous peine de ridicule).

*

Ne lisez pas de médiocrités. Lisez les œuvres des grands esprits et concourez avec eux. Ou bien instruisez-vous…, cultivez votre mémoire. La mémoire est la clef de tout, croyez-moi.

*

C'est une manie de l'époque depuis les dessins de Victor Hugo d'avoir plusieurs arts à la fois. Une vie d'homme est insuffisante pour un seul art. Surtout quand on a un métier par-dessus le marché. Laissez donc de côté musique, peinture et danse. J'ai perdu ma vie littéraire à cause de la peinture et perdu ma vie picturale à cause de la littérature. Maintenant tout est fini. Bon débarras!

*

This link is everything. You can produce brilliant exercises and also be a permeable, sad man, but if the exercises do not express the permeable man, you remain divided and devoid of interest. Then people say, 'He's not sincere,' a word that doesn't mean much in the mouth of fools, but means a great deal in the mouth of one who knows.

*

Don't be bored. Boredom is a mortal sin as far as poetry is concerned. Boredom is the hell of poetry ... unless it's a fine boredom, the boredom of Byron, who had made the round of the sciences, society, the earth, languages and love.

But that boredom is so rare that it's best not to speak of it (for fear of ridicule).

*

Don't read mediocrities. Read the works of great minds and compete with them. Or else educate yourself..., cultivate your memory. Memory is the key to everything, believe me.

*

It's a craze of the period since the drawings of Victor Hugo to practise several arts at the same time. A man's life isn't long enough for one art. Especially when one has to earn one's living into the bargain. So leave aside music, painting and dance. I've wasted my literary life because of painting and lost my life as a painter because of literature. Now that's all over. Good riddance!

*

Ennuyez-vous. Car ce jour-là vous prendrez un porte-plume et un papier et vous ferez peut-être un chef-d'œuvre. Tout est dans la qualité de l'ennui.

*

Il ne faut pas travailler tout le temps. Il faut prendre du temps, prendre son temps. Il faut digérer. Oui. C'est dans la digestion des connaissances que réside le talent. L'essentiel est de n'avoir pas de minutes vulgaires ou insignifiantes.

*

Aimer les mots. Aimer un mot. Le répéter, s'en gargariser. Comme un peintre aime une ligne, une forme, une couleur. (TRÈS IMPORTANT.)

*

Autour d'un mot, se coagule une phrase, un vers, une strophe, une idée.
   Ah! quel beau mode d'extériorisation! Et extérioriser, c'est tout.

*

Extérioriser!
   Une œuvre est une île lointaine. On y va en bateau, en avion. Elle est là-bas.
   Que cette œuvre soit un quatrain ou une tragédie. Comment extérioriser?

*

Sans doute par la quantité d'idées, de sentiments qui se sont incendiés pour la produire?

*

Be bored. For that day you will take pen and paper and perhaps you will write a masterpiece. It all depends on the quality of the boredom.

*

You don't have to work all the time. You must take time, take your own time. You must digest. Yes. Talent dwells in the digestion of knowledge. The essential is not to have any moments that are vulgar or meaningless.

*

Love words. Love a word. Repeat it, gargle with it. As a painter loves a line, a form, a colour. (VERY IMPORTANT).

*

Around a word coagulates a phrase, a line, a stanza, an idea.

What a fine way to exteriorise! And exteriorising is everything.

*

Exteriorising!

A work is a distant isle. One goes there by boat, by plane. It's over there.

Be that work a quatrain or a tragedy. How is one to exteriorise?

*

No doubt by the quantity of ideas, of feelings burnt up to produce it?

*

Ou bien parce qu'elle s'attache à un pivot qui n'est pas en vous.

*

Cherchez à extérioriser. Chacun a sa méthode. Les points de départ dans l'érudition? oui – ou dans l'observation d'un cas humain? oui.

Je n'en sais rien. Ça colle tout de suite au fond du plat parce qu'il n'y avait pas de beurre. Je crois que les œuvres très extériorisées sont très rares. Balzac, c'est toujours lui qui parle. Je suis mauvais critique.

Ce qui est très inventé est par le fait extériorisé. (Les comédies de Musset sont extériorisées) (Shakespeare aussi). Le style c'est d'extérioriser(?).

A vous d'y penser: je vous indique des portes. Un jour c'est vous qui m'éclairerez ou qui, même, vous moquerez de moi (mais oui, mais oui).

Les très grands esprits comme Edgar Poe extériorisent naturellement.

*

Bien entendu, le public s'en fout. Mais nous ne travaillons pas pour le public ou bien si nous travaillons pour le public, il faut tout changer. Il faut alors étudier son goût et le servir mot par mot: lui parler de ses sales passions et sombrer avec en enfer.

*

Ne méprisez pas les articles des critiques. Vous verrez ce qu'on loue d'un auteur et ce qu'on lui reproche. Cependant méfiez-vous, car il y a infiniment peu de bons critiques. Critiquez le critique. Ayez confiance dans votre personnalité quand elle sera formée, dans dix ou vingt ans.

*

Or else because it's attached to a pivot that's not in you.

*

Try to exteriorise. Each one has his own method. Points of departure in erudition? Yes. Or in the observation of a human case? Yes.

I just don't know. It sticks straight away to the bottom of the dish because there was no butter. I think that very exteriorised works are very rare. With Balzac it's always himself speaking. I'm a poor critic.

What shows a lot of invention is exteriorised ipso facto (The comedies of Musset are exteriorised) (Shakespeare too).

Style is exteriorising (?)

Think about it yourself: I am showing you ways in. One day it will be your turn to guide me or even to make fun of me (yes. oh yes).

Very great minds like Edgar Poe exteriorise naturally.

*

Of course the public doesn't give a damn. But we're not working for the public, or else if we are working for the public everything has to be changed. Then the public's taste will have to be studied and served word by word: we shall have to speak to it of its dirty passions and founder with it in Hell.

*

Don't scorn the critics' articles. You will see what in an author earns praise and what earns reproaches. However, don't trust them, for there is an infinitesimal number of good critics. Criticise the critic. Have confidence in your personality when it's formed, ten or twenty years from now.

*

On prône beaucoup les «œuvres de jeunesse». Je suis d'un avis contraire.

Des œuvres de jeunesse sont un remords vivant (encore heureux quand il n'est pas vivant, c'est-à-dire que l'œuvre est oubliée, pourrie). Si vous saviez la douleur que c'est de trouver stupide l'élucubration commise il y a trente ans, surtout quand par-dessus le marché elle est prétentieuse. Je crois qu'il faut attendre... attendre...

*

On me dit là-dessus: oui, mais vous êtes d'une époque qui a sa couleur. Si vous ne parlez pas, un autre parlera avant vous. Or je prétends que c'est justement cette couleur de l'époque, c'est-à-dire la mode, qui est mauvaise. Ce qui est bon en vous, c'est ce qui est éternel, vous avez le temps de le dire. Cervantès a écrit le Quichotte à 60 ans, et Jean-Jacques n'a rien écrit avant 40. Formez-vous avant d'écrire.

*

Travailler. C'est vite dit. C'est le «comment» qui est tout. Le «qui» Le «quoi?» Le «pourquoi?»

*

Le premier geste du travail est la *séparation*. Il faut, présent et visible, se séparer de ce qui est présent et visible. Creuser un abîme entre le toi et le moi, bâtir une citadelle du moi – quand cet abîme sera creusé vous aurez déjà bien travaillé: il y faut du temps et une application minutieuse.

*

'Works of youth' are widely extolled. I'm of the contrary opinion.

A work of youth is a living reproach (great relief when it is no longer living, that is to say, when the work is forgotten, rotted away). If you knew what anguish it is to find the lucubration stupid that you committed thirty years ago, above all when it's pretentious into the bargain. I think one must wait... wait...

*

On that subject people say to me, 'Yes, but you are of an age which has its character. If you don't speak another will speak before you.' Now, I claim that it's precisely this character of the age, that is to say, fashion, which is bad. What's good in you is what's eternal; you've time to say it. Cervantes wrote *Don Quixote* at sixty, and Jean-Jacques wrote nothing before he was 40. Train yourself before you write.

*

Work. That's easily said. The 'how' is everything. The 'who?' The 'what?' The 'why?'

*

The first gesture of work is *separation*. Present and visible, you must separate yourself from what is present and visible. Dig a gulf between the Thou and the I, build a citadel of the I. When this gulf is dug you will already have done some good work: it needs time and a meticulous application.

*

Le deuxième geste du travail est le *silence*. Quoi! Vous allez encourager ces conversations absurdes et insignifiantes en vous y mêlant?

Ou bien allez-vous faire le professeur et enseigner à ces gens que leurs conversations sont absurdes.

Eh bien! Taisez-vous.

*

Le troisième geste du travail est *l'ignorance*. L'ignorance avec une formidable érudition. Dès le premier mot érudit, posez-vous la question: «Le sait-il? Comment le sait-il? D'où lui vient cette connaissance?» De là, une révision constante des valeurs. Alors, vous viendra cet éclat de rire que suggèrent le monde, la science, la philosophie, les sciences, les philosophies. Cet éclat de rire est la sagesse, qui est l'escalier vers Dieu.

*

(N'allez surtout pas croire que je suis ainsi. Mais ce que je ne sais pas faire, vous le saurez peut-être.)

*

Éclat de rire. Entendons-nous. Ne cherchez pas à vous moquer. Attendez que la moquerie vienne d'elle-même et *malgré vous*. La moquerie est un péché grave, mais la gravité isolée est une vertu qui ne peut empêcher la moquerie.

*

Que l'indulgence et la charité corrigent le jugement trop raide.

Ce mélange de pitié et de justice est le fond d'un talent chrétien, c'est-à-dire modeste.

The second gesture of work is *silence*. What! Do you mean to encourage those absurd and insignificant conversations by get-ting involved in them?

Or else do you mean to play the schoolmaster and teach these people that their conversations are absurd? Well then! Shut up.

*

The third gesture of work is *ignorance*. Ignorance with a formidable learning. From the first learned word set yourself the questions, 'Does he know? How does he know? From where does he get that knowledge?' Thence comes a constant revision of values. Then you will be visited by that explosion of laughter suggested by society, science, philosophy, the sciences, the philosophies. That explosion of laughter is wisdom, which is the stairway towards God.

*

(Above all, don't think that I am like that. But what I can't do, you may be able to).

*

Explosion of laughter. Let's get this clear. Don't try to mock. Wait until mockery comes of itself and *in spite of you*. Mockery is a grave sin, but detached gravity is a virtue which cannot prevent mockery.

*

When judgment is too rigid, let it be corrected by indulgence and charity.

This mixture of pity and justice is the basis of a Christian   that is to say, a modest   talent.

Le geste de la sublime ignorance est l'étonnement. L'étonnement est la candeur et la candeur est la route de toutes les découvertes en art comme en science. «Laissez venir à moi les petits enfants car le Paradis est à ceux qui leur ressemblent.» Or le Paradis est *aussi* sur terre. Le Paradis est la sagesse.

*

A propos de chasteté.

Savez-vous qu'il est ordonné aux magiciens de ne faire aucune opération avant le quarantième jour après le coït (volontaire ou non).

Or une œuvre d'art est une opération magique. Sans commentaires.

*

Balzac disait: «Une nuit d'amour, c'est un livre de moins.»

*

Vénus poursuivie par le démon Typhon, se réfugie auprès de Mercure (ou de Neptune), qui est l'Esprit.

*

Rapports entre l'amour charnel et la force morale. Je ne connais pas la physiologie. Célibat des prêtres dans les religions sérieuses. (Je ne parle pas du protestantisme qui est sans mystique et une morale seulement.)

*

The gesture of sublime ignorance is wonder. Wonder is candour and candour is the road to all discoveries in art as in science. 'Suffer the little children to come unto me, for of such is the Kingdom of Heaven.' Now, Heaven is also on earth. Heaven is wisdom.

*

About chastity.

Do you know that magicians are commanded to perform no operation before the fortieth day after coitus (voluntary or not)?

Now, a work of art is a magical operation. No comment.

*

Balzac said, 'One night of love, one less book.'

*

Venus pursued by the demon Typhon takes refuge with Mercury (or with Neptune), who is the Spirit.

*

Relations between carnal love and moral strength. I don't know any physiology. Celibacy of priests in serious religions. (I'm not speaking of Protestantism, which has no mysticism and is only a moral philosophy).

*

Un littérateur est un juge d'instruction, un confesseur, un commissaire de police.

*

Allez au tribunal. Allez à la cour d'assises. Vous y verrez l'humanité aussi nue qu'un malade.

*

Prenez des notes tous les jours, d'une façon nette, lisible, avec des dates soigneuses. Si j'avais écrit le journal de ma vie au jour le jour, j'aurais aujourd'hui le dictionnaire Larousse. Un mot écouté, recueilli, et voilà toute une atmosphère reconstituée. Ah! Tout ce qu'on perd! Toutes les perles perdues! Écrivez le journal de votre vie:

«Aujourd'hui 22 juin, étudié les os de la jambe. Ma concierge dit: «Dans les banques, on verse l'argent à contre-goutte». Le professeur X a un grand nez comme François Ier, il se caresse la barbe et fait le beau pour plaire aux étudiantes, etc... Lu tel livre sur telle question. Retenu telle chose. Mangé avec un tel (son portrait).

Passé à la cour d'assises; on jugeait telle affaire (rapporter l'affaire).»

*

Il est bon d'analyser des romans même mauvais pour voir comment c'est fait et pouvoir en faire autant en mieux.

*

Aller le moins possible dans le monde. Tous y ont un masque. On n'apprend absolument rien dans le monde. Ou ce qu'on y apprend ne vaut pas le temps qu'on y perd.

A man of letters is an examining magistrate, a confessor, a commissioner of police.

*

Go to the court. Go to the assizes. There you will see humanity stripped like a sick man.

*

Take notes every day, notes that are clear, readable and carefully dated. If I had written the journal of my life from day to day I should now have the Larousse dictionary. You hear a word, you collect it, and there you have the reconstitution of a whole atmosphere. Oh, all the things you lose! All those lost pearls! Write the journal of your life:

"Today, 22nd June, studied the bones of the leg. My concierge says, 'In the banks they pour money up the spout.' Professor X has a big nose like Francis I, he strokes his beard and shows himself off to attract the girl students, etc... Read such and such a book on such and such a question. Remembered such and such a thing. Ate with such and such a person (his portrait). Went to the assizes; such and such a case was being tried (give an account of the case)."

*

It's good to analyse even bad novels, in order to see what makes them bad and to be able to do so much better.

*

Go as little as possible into society. Everybody there wears a mask. In society you learn absolutely nothing. Or what you do learn isn't worth the time you waste. Don't dine

Ne pas dîner en ville surtout à votre âge qui est celui de l'étude. Le monde n'est qu'une stupide séduction. Vous le verrez bien suffisamment à son chevet de malades. On vous invitera pour dire: «Nous avions J. E.» Ils sont très friands de jeunes intellectuels, et ils ne se doutent pas qu'ils sont la cause de vies manquées, d'œuvres superficielles, d'examens ratés, les assassins... on prétextera des cousinages, des fiançailles, etc., refusez tout impitoyablement. Je vous recommande dix ans d'égoïsme, d'indépendance folle, de raideur énorme.

*

Souvenez-vous à jamais de cette parole:

«Au début de toute carrière, il y a un *miracle de travail.*»

Et travail veut dire solitude.

*

La question du style.

«Le style c'est l'homme même», dit Buffon, ce qui veut dire: ce qu'il y a de plus profond dans la poitrine et dans le sang de l'homme.

Il faut écrire avec l'inaliénable de l'homme; là est l'originalité (l'origine), l'originalité non cherchée mais naturelle de l'homme même.

J'ai déjà parlé des clichés plus haut. La grande affaire est de modeler son idée avec des mots, son sentiment avec une syntaxe. Se mettre devant l'objet et attendre que l'épithète qui le décrit arrive.

*

On m'a enseigné ceci au collège:

1° diviser son sujet en paragraphes, en réservant le plus important pour le milieu et en dégradant vers la fin.

in town, especially at your age, which is the age for study. Society is only a stupid seduction. You will see quite enough of it at the bedside of its sick. You will be invited so that they can say, 'We had J. E.' They are very partial to young intellectuals and they don't suspect that they are the cause of spoilt lives, superficial works, failed examinations, the murderers... They will plead relationships, engagements to be married etc. Refuse all, ruthlessly, I recommend ten years of egotism, mad independence, atrocious inflexibility.

*

Forever remember this saying:
    'At the beginning of every career there is a miracle of work'.
    And work means solitude.

*

The question of style.
    'Style is the man,' said Buffon, which means: what is most pro-found in the breast and in the blood of man.
    You must write with what is inalienable in man; there lies originality (the origin), effortless originality natural to man.
    I've already spoken of clichés, The great thing is to mould your idea with words, your feeling with syntax. Take up your position in front of the object and wait for the arrival of the epithet that describes it.

*

They taught me this at college:
    1. Divide your subject into paragraphs, keeping the most important for the middle and graduating towards the end.

2° un paragraphe pour le thème le développe et conclut en reprenant la première phrase sous une autre forme.

Je ne me moque pas du tout de cet enseignement; c'est là que malgré toutes les fantaisies, il faut revenir... je parlerai du développement plus loin.

*

Il y a la cadence même de la prose; il y a le leit-motiv plus ou moins voilé qui donne l'unité. Je parlerai du leit-motiv.

Dans un roman le leit-motiv, c'est les types qui reviennent avec leur caractère uniforme ou évolué (un roman mauvais est un roman où les caractères n'évoluent pas).

*

M.X. me dit un jour: «Le dialogue s'écrit moins.» Ah! quelle bêtise! Le dialogue s'écrit davantage, car un personnage parle son propre langage, et voilà bien le cas de surveiller ce langage! il ne faut lui mettre dans la bouche que ce qui peut en sortir.

Une dame avare dit:

«Prenez une chaise. Ça ne coûte rien, ce n'est pas comme à l'église.»

Une dame douillette dit:

«Asseyez-vous dans ce fauteuil, il est très bon.»

Une dame à l'étiquette dit:

«Une chaise? mais non. Un fauteuil.» Etc...

Vous voyez qu'il faut choisir les mots du dialogue, c'est-à-dire *l'écrire*. Car le choix c'est le style.

Un orgueilleux doré se sert de mots orgueilleux et dorés. Un prêtre parle comme un prêtre, un ouvrier comme un ouvrier. Certes. Le langage professionnel est une source de comique certain.

Vous savez tout cela. Mais j'ignore ce que vous ignorez; j'écris à bâtons rompus, confiant dans l'espoir que je vous

2. A paragraph develops the theme and ends by taking up the first sentence again in another form.

I'm certainly not scoffing at this teaching; for all one's whims one has to come back to it... I shall speak of development farther on.

*

Even prose has its cadence; there is the leitmotiv, more or less concealed, which gives unity. I shall speak of the leitmotiv.

In a novel the leitmotiv consists of the persons reappearing with their characters uniform or evolved (a bad novel is a novel where the characters do not evolve).

*

Monsieur X said to me one day, 'Dialogue is less trouble to write.' What a silly remark! Dialogue is more trouble to write, for a character speaks in his own style and you must keep a check on that style! You must put in the mouth only what can come out of it.

A mean lady says:

'Take a chair. It doesn't cost anything, it isn't like at church.'

A sensitive lady says:

'Sit in that armchair, it's very comfortable.'

A polite lady says:

'A chair? Oh, no! An armchair.' Etc...

You see that you have to choose the words of the dialogue, that is to say, write it. For choice is style.

A rich, proud man will use rich, proud words. A priest speaks like a priest, a workman like a workman. Of course. Professional language is a sure source of comedy.

You know all that. But I don't know what you don't know; I'm writing by fits and starts, confident in the hope

ferai réfléchir sur tel point si je vous agace ailleurs.

*

Méfiez-vous de votre propre caractère en prose et servez-vous de tout le dictionnaire sans préférence. Vos personnages ne doivent pas vous ressembler ou vous ressembler le moins possible. C'est à eux-mêmes qu'ils ressemblent. Or vos mots ne doivent pas être «vous», *mais eux*. De même, ce n'est pas l'objet que vous aimez que vous décrivez mais l'objet qu'ils aiment, eux, et des paysages adéquats à la situation, la leur. Or vos mots décrivent ce qui est à vous, mais non ce qui est à eux. – Donc attention!

*

Un exemple. Dans la ballade du corbeau d'Edgar Poe, il y a une lampe, un fauteuil de velours violet, un buste de Pallas, une nuit de méditation et d'étude. Voyez comme le décor est arrangé pour le maximum d'effet. Quel modèle! Il faut savoir quel effet on veut produire et disposer tout en vue de cet effet.

*

L'art n'est jamais qu'un effet à produire. Il faut s'interroger là-dessus. Vous n'allez pas parler de velours si vous voulez décrire la misère des quartiers de Paris. A moins que vous ne vouliez un contraste.

Choisissez donc des détails caractéristiques. A ce sujet, étudiez des romans russes. Je vous recommande *Les Âmes mortes* de Gogol. Vous y verrez comment on peint un caractère par l'aspect d'une maison ou d'un mobilier.

*

that I shall make you ponder such and such a point if I irritate you elsewhere.

*

Distrust your own personality in prose and make use of the whole dictionary without preference. Your characters must not be like you or they must be as little like you as possible. They are like themselves. Now, your words must not be 'you', but them. Likewise, it's not the object you love that you're describing but the object they love and landscapes right for the situation, which is theirs. Now, your words describe what is yours, but not what is theirs. So take care!

*

An example. In Edgar Poe's ballad, *The Raven*, there is a lamp, an armchair of violet velvet, a bust of Pallas, a night of meditation and study. See how the decor is arranged for maximum effect. What a model! You need to know what effect you want to produce and set out everything with that effect in view.

*

Art is never only an effect to be produced. You must examine yourself on that. You're not going to talk about velvet if you mean to describe the poverty-stricken quarters of Paris. Unless you want a contrast.

Then choose characteristic details. On this subject study Russian novels. I recommend Gogol's *Dead Souls*. There you will see how a character is depicted by the look of a house or furniture.

*

Ayez des caractères dans la tête. Pensez-y, poussez-les au *type*. Car il n'y a d'intérêt que dans le général. Il faut que chacun se reconnaisse ou reconnaisse ses proches dans vos personnages.

*

Manière de graduer l'intérêt, d'attacher le lecteur... Ça, je ne sais pas... Étudiez Balzac, c'est le maître du roman passionnant et plutôt Dostoievsky.
Lisez beaucoup, lisez lentement, prenez des notes.

*

Il faut posséder en deux mots un caractère dans son infinie variété; le posséder pour le faire vivre en le prenant par n'importe quel bout. L'opposer à ses voisins et assister à ses actions et réactions, de sorte qu'on ne fait pas le roman, ce sont des caractères qui le font.

*

Le développement.
Savoir développer, c'est d'une importance essentielle.
Développer, c'est comprendre, c'est analyser sa propre pensée.
Développer. Tout l'art, quel qu'il soit, est dans ce mot. On développe un thème musical; la *VIe Symphonie* est le développement du chant du coucou. Un tableau de peintures est une parabole développée. Un cercle est le développement d'un dodécagone, et le cercle lui-même par les tangentes devient un autre polygone.
Une plante est le développement d'une graine. Un paragraphe est le développement d'une pensée et le chapitre est le développement du paragraphe. Le livre est le développement des chapitres. Une petite idée bien creusée donne 400 pages dans une œuvre classiquement

Have characters in your head. Think about it, knock them into types. For only the general is interesting. In your characters everyone must recognise himself or those near to him.

*

How to raise the interest by degrees, to catch the reader's attention ... I don't know about that ... Study Balzac, he's the master of the novel of strong emotions, or rather Dostoyevsky.

Read widely, read slowly, take notes.

*

A few words must hold a character in its infinite variety; hold it to give it life, taking it at any point. Putting it in opposition to its neighbours and witnessing its actions and reactions, so that one doesn't make the novel, it's made by the characters themselves.

*

Development.

It's essential to know how to develop.

Developing is understanding, it's analysing your own thought. Developing. All art, of whatever sort, is in that word. A musical theme is developed; the 6th Symphony is the development of the song of the cuckoo. A painting is a developed parable. A circle is the development of a dodecagon, and by 'its tangents the circle itself becomes another polygon.

A plant is the development of a seed. A paragraph is the development of a thought and the chapter is the development of the paragraph. The book is the development of the chapters. Thoroughly examined a little idea

composée.

Pourquoi un caractère humain ne peut-il être le développement d'un seul principe?

Je dois dire à la vérité qu'il y a peu de caractères vivants dans la littérature française à cause de ce principe du développement.

On a appliqué le principe de rhétorique du développement à l'âme humaine alors que l'âme humaine n'y répond pas. On a dit: Il y a l'avare, le misanthrope, le jaloux, et on a marché.

Malheureusement, ce n'est pas ça. L'âme humaine est une, mais ses appels extérieurs sont nombreux et les esprits inspirateurs se répondent mutuellement. Il y a divinement une seule âme mais combien d'esprits extérieurs, combien d'influences?

En sorte qu'un caractère n'a pas d'unité, quoiqu'on lui en impose une.

De là la difficulté de développer un caractère. Tout se développe sauf le caractère humain! il s'expose tant bien que mal et évolue…

O malheureuse rhétorique! comme on construit un livre sur une idée ou sur une intrigue, on est obligé de soumettre des héros à cette idée ou à cette intrigue. De là bien peu d'étude psychologique de l'homme.

*

Un beau roman serait celui qui, animé d'une profonde vérité humaine générale bien sentie, contiendrait des caractères justes et complets qui contribueraient à l'illustration de cette vérité psychologique. *Germinal* de Zola est un beau roman; *Boule de suif* de Maupassant est un beau conte. *Madame Bovary* est un bon roman. Mais je préfère *Les Possédés* de Dostoievsky, œuvre de génie, ou *Les Karamasof.*

*

gives 400 pages in a work classically composed.

Why can't a human character be the development of a single principle?

It must indeed be said that there are few living characters in French literature because of this principle of development.

The rhetorical principle of development has been applied to the human soul when the human soul does not conform to it. They said, 'There is the miser, the misanthrope, the jealous husband,' and off they went.

Unfortunately, it's not like that. The human soul is one, but the exterior calls on it are numerous and the inspiring spirits reply each to each. Divinely there is a single soul, but how many exterior spirits, how many influences?

So that a character has no unity, although a unity is imposed on it. Hence the difficulty in developing a character. Everything develops save the human character! It explains itself as best it can and evolves...

On, wretched rhetoric! As one constructs a book on an idea or a plot, one is obliged to subordinate heroes to this idea or that plot. That is why there is precious little psychological study of man.

*

A fine novel would be one which, animated by a general human truth which was profound and profoundly felt, contained apt and whole characters that contributed to the illustration of that psychological truth. Zola's *Germinal* is a fine novel; Maupassant's *Boule de suif* is a fine tale. *Madame Bovary* is a good novel. But I prefer Dostoyevsky's *The Possessed,* a work of genius, or *The Brothers Karamazov.*

*

Il y a des œuvres qui valent par la curiosité ou la révélation du tempérament de l'auteur.

*

Un roman est le développement d'une idée par les personnages qui y luttent entre eux. Je ne parle pas du roman à thèse.

*

On fait ce qu'on peut. Mais encore faut-il savoir *de quoi il s'agit.*

*

Molière dit: «Le tout est de plaire et de toucher.» Certes. Il ne faut pas tendre à faire un chef-d'œuvre. Il y a chef-d'œuvre sans qu'on le veuille. On le rate pour l'avoir voulu tel. Il y a des œuvres dont l'immortalité dépend du hasard. Une belle vieille chanson a survécu; de beaucoup plus belles ont péri. Pourquoi? On trouve un manuscrit copte; on n'en a qu'un; il est immortel. Espérons que telle de nos œuvres aura cette chance.

*

C'est en étudiant *Britannicus* que Cocteau est devenu auteur dramatique *(sic).*

*

Chaque caractère a son secret moteur, bien éloigné de l'apparence. Mon ami R.F. était censément architecte, en réalité il était acrobate (de cirque). Mme X., hôtelière en Bretagne, est impératrice. M.Z., propriétaire foncier, est en réalité un petit enfant, fou de vanité et capable de

There are works whose worth is in their curiosity or their revelation of the author's temperament.

*

A novel is the development of an idea by the characters contending in it. I'm not speaking of the *roman à thèse*.

*

One does what one can. But still one needs to know *what it's all about.*

*

Molière said, 'Pleasing and touching are everything.' Most certainly. You needn't strain yourself to create a master-piece. Masterpieces come without your trying. You make a mess of it by trying. There are works whose immortali-ty depends on chance. A beautiful old song has survived; some that were much more beautiful have perished. Why? A Coptic manuscript is found; there's only one; it's immor-tal. Let us hope that such of our works will have this luck.

*

It was by studying *Britannicus* that Cocteau became a dra-matic author *(sic)*.

*

Each character has his motive secret, far removed from appearance. My friend R.F. was supposedly an architect; in reality he was an acrobat (in a circus). Madame X., ho-tel-keeper in Brittany, is an empress. Monsieur Z., land-owner, is really a little child, mad with vanity and capa-

compromettre sa fortune entière pour placer un mot qu'il croit «seigneurial». M.X., qu'on nomme académicien, est naturellement mendiant, habile mendiant et parasite.

Il s'agit de trouver le mot, le mot moteur.

Il s'agit de confronter des caractères.

*

Je pense que ces pensées (?) sont ou trop claires ou trop obscures. Excusez les unes et demandez l'explication des autres. Je suis à votre disposition. Remerciez vos parents de leur accueil et présentez-leur mes hommages.

MAX JACOB

ble of jeopardising his whole fortune to put in a word he thinks 'lordly'. Monsieur X., elected Academician, is by nature a beggar, a clever beggar and parasite.

It's a question of finding the word, the motive word.

It's a question of confronting characters.

*

I think that these thoughts (?) are either too clear or too obscure. Forgive the one and ask for an explanation of the other. I'm at your disposal. Thank your parents for their welcome and convey my respects.

MAX JACOB

On appelle «vraisemblance», ce qui est le cliché habituel des médiocres. La vérité n'est que rarement vraisemblable. Est-il vraisemblable qu'une petite crapule que personne ne voulait fréquenter soit devenue ministre d'État?

Rimbaud, Lautréamont, Laforgue, Verlaine, Corbière très bien, il y a 50 ans: J'attends J. E.

Faire beaucoup de pastiches volontaires pour être sûr de n'en pas faire d'involontaires.

C'est à vous de faire des pensées avec mes pauvres conseils: Moi je n'en ai ni le temps ni le courage. Relisez-les plusieurs fois et excusez ma bêtise notoire. Au revoir.

Supplément pour répondre à une question d'ailleurs embarrassante. Qu'est-ce que le "vers lyrique?

Je n'en sais rien ou ça serait trop long à expliquer.

*

Le lyrisme est un état de pensée sans penser, de sentiments sans sentiments, prêt à nourrir une expression harmonieuse.

Les mots qui viennent alors sont dits lyriques.

*

Je crois que c'est tout.

*

Le propre du lyrisme est l'inconscience, mais une inconscience surveillée.

*

Il peut y avoir lyrisme ailleurs qu'en poésie mais il n'y a pas de poésie vraie sans lyrisme.

*

What they call 'probability' is the customary cliche of me-
diocre people. Truth is only rarely probable. Is it probable
that a little louse nobody wanted to keep company with
should have become Minister of State?

Rimbaud, Lautréamont, Laforgue, Verlaine, Corbière
were all very well 50 years ago. I'm waiting for J. E.

Write a lot of intentional pastiches, to make sure you
don't write them unintentionally.

It's for you to do some thinking over my poor advice:
I have neither the time nor the courage. Re-read it several
times and forgive my notorious silliness. Good-bye.

Supplement in order to reply to an embarrassing
question. What is the lyrical line?

I don't know, or that would take too long to explain.

*

Lyricism is a state of thought without thinking, of feelings
without feelings, ready to nourish a harmonious expres-
sion.

Words which come then are said to be lyrical.

*

I think that's all.

*

Lyricism belongs to the unconscious, but an unconscious
under supervision.

*

There can be lyricism elsewhere than in poetry, but
there's no real poetry without lyricism.

*

69

Le lyrisme à l'état pur se trouve dans quelques romances populaires et dans les contes d'enfants.

*

Un œuf très grand descend en moi, très profondément, cette descente est accompagnée d'un flux montant d'étincelles lyriques. Ces étincelles sont des mots, des associations de mots.

Saint-Benoît-sur-Loire, 23 juin '41.

Lyricism in its pure state is found in a few folk-ballads and in children's tales.

*

A very big egg descends in me, descends very deep, accompanied by a rising flood of lyrical sparks. These sparks are words, associations of words.

Saint-Benoît-sur-Loire, 23 June '41

EN APPENDICE

Extraits d'une Lettre à X

Si j'avais aujourd'hui, ... août 1943, a former un poète je ne lui dirais pas comme j'ai dit en 37, à M.B.: «Utilise tes rêves de la nuit. Écris comme une cuisinière et place tous les mots de la langue usuelle sur cette table de hachoir!» Non! je lui dirais seulement ceci:

1° N'écris pas avec des mots, écris avec des objets et *avec des SENTIMENTS* (donc: *fuis à jamais tout langage critique, tout langage intellectuel et même la description et le récit)*;

2° N'écris pas une seule phrase qui ait la forme de la précédente, à moins d'une ferme volonté de rythme spécial, mais varie ta syntaxe comme Shakespeare varie sa syntaxe, collectionne ces formes syntaxiques, tiens-en un répertoire, un registre. *Les idées viennent seules quand le moule est prêt à les recevoir.* C'est le secret de ne jamais ennuyer;

3° et ceci est le plus important: une œuvre ne vaut pas par ce qu'elle contient, mais par ce qui l'environne. Il faut que les mots «Bonjour, Bonsoir!» soient environnés par une immense philosophie de la nature, de la société, de l'astronomie, de la métaphysique, etc. C'est le secret des grandes œuvres. C'est aussi le secret de l'humble folklore lequel résume un peuple, son histoire, etc. Ibsen, mais oui! Goethe, Tolstoï, Diderot (?) et quelques autres valent par là et ne sont pas des fabricants comme Hugo, Zola et même le GÉNIAL et admiré Dostoievsky.

APPENDIX

Extracts from a Letter to X

If today, ... August 1943, I had to train a poet, I shouldn't tell him as I told M.B. in '37, 'Use the dreams that come to you in the night. Write like a cook and place all the words of everyday speech on that chopping-table!' No! I should tell him only this:

1. Don't write with words, write with objects and *with FEELINGS* (then: *avoid for ever all critical language, all intellectual language and even description and narrative*).

2. Don't write a single sentence constructed like the one before, unless you firmly intend a special rhythm, but vary your syntax as Shakespeare varies his syntax, collect those syntactic forms, keep a repertory of them, a register. *Ideas come of themselves when the mould is ready to receive them.* It's the secret of never being boring.

3. And this is the most important: the value of a work is not in what it contains but in what surrounds it. The words *Good morning! Good evening!* must be surrounded with an immense philosophy of Nature, Society, astronomy, metaphysics, etc. That is the secret of great works. It's also the secret of the humble folklore which sums up a people, its history, etc. Ibsen, indeed yes! Goethe, Tolstoy, Diderot (?) and some others have that sort of value and aren't manufacturers like Hugo, Zola and even the INGENIOUS and admired Dostoyevsky.

Translator's Notes

1 Joseph Prudhomme, a prosperous bourgeois, was the creation of Henry Monnier (1799–1877), author, actor and caricaturist. In the comedy *Grandeur et Decadence de M Joseph Prudhomme* (1852) a servant says of him that as soon as he wakes in the morning he calls for his newspaper, to find out what he thinks today.

2 Monsieur Homais is the opinionated local apothecary in Flaubert's *Madame Bovary*. His face, we are told, 'expressed nothing but self-satisfaction.'

3 *Voie lactée, ô sœur lumineuse*
   des blancs ruisseaux de Chanaan.

   In this quotation from Guillaume Apollinaire's *La chanson du mal aimé* Max Jacob has restored the punctuation, which Apollinaire suppressed.

4 The French text runs: 'Ma concierge dit: «Dans les banques, on verse l'argent à contre-goutte». Obviously, this could not be translated word for word.

5 M.B. is Marcel Béalu, poet, bookseller, and editor of *Conseils à un jeune poète*. (Gallimard 1945).

Un 'Jeune Poète' Parle...

J'ai rencontré Max Jacob en Juin 1941, au début de ce bel été qui nous paraissait, en France, un entracte de la guerre. Je venais d'avoir 17 ans et je commençais, selon le vœu de mon père, des études de médecine, alors que j'aurais préféré de beaucoup une carrière plus 'littéraire'. En effet, depuis quelques années déjà, j'avais le goût d'écrire et j'avais composé quelques vers, assez malhabiles bien sûr.

Aussi fus-je ravi lorsqu'on m'annonça la prochaine visite de Max Jacob, invité par un ami commun, le Docteur Robert S., qui le connaissait de longue date. J'avais déjà entrevu Max Jacob au cours d'une promenade à Saint-Benoît-sur-Loire et j'étais curieux de rencontrer cet étrange personnage dont la légende, la vie, la silhouette ne pouvaient qu'exciter ma curiosité. Je ne savais pas grand-chose de lui et je n'avais lu aucun de ses livres, qui – fou t-il le rappeler – n'avaient à l'époque qu'une audience des plus restreintes.

Le repas, qui concernait beaucoup plus mes parents et leurs hôtes que moi-même, ne m'a laissé aucun souvenir. De tels dîners, entre gens de bonne compagnie, n'étaient pas rares à la maison et d'autres artistes, peintres et musiciens, plus ou moins célèbres, s'étaient déjà assis à notre table. La conversation fut sans doute, comme à l'habitude, aimable et spirituelle, Max Jacob fut sans doute brillant, mais rien ne serait resté de cette soirée si je ne lui avais fourni innocemment le prétexte de rédiger son 'Art Poétique'. J'étais alors entré, sans le savoir et par une toute petite porte, dans l'histoire littéraire!

Quelques semaines plus tard, fidèle à sa promesse, Max Jacob me faisait parvenir un cahier d'écolier à couverture rouge, sur laquelle il avait écrit mon nom. En 35 pages, d'une fine écriture serrée, il avait rédigé une sorte de journal intellectuel, plus monologue intérieur

A 'Young Poet' Speaks...

I met Max Jacob in June 1941, at the beginning of that beautiful summer which in France seemed to us an interlude in the war. I was just seventeen and, following my father's wish, I was starting to study medicine, though I would have much preferred a career that was more 'literary'. Indeed, for the last few years I had had an inclination to write and I had composed a few verses, rather clumsy work to be sure.

So it was that I was delighted when I was told of the forthcoming visit of Max Jacob, invited by a mutual friend, Dr. Robert S., an old acquaintance of his. I had already caught a glimpse of Max Jacob during a walk at Saint-Benoît-sur-Loire and I was keen to meet this strange individual whose legend, life, silhouette could not fail to amuse my curiosity. I didn't know much about him and I had read none of his books, which it must be remembered, had at that time only the most restricted readership.

Of the meal, which concerned my parents and their guests far more than it concerned me, nothing remains in my memory. Such dinners, among good company, were not infrequent at home, and other artists, painters and musicians, more or less famous, had already sat down at our table. Doubtless the conversation was, as usual, pleasant and witty, doubtless Max Jacob was brilliant, but nothing would have remained of that evening had I not innocently provided him with a pretext for drafting his 'Art of Poetry'. So without knowing it and by a tiny door I had entered literary history!

Some weeks later, true to his promise, Max Jacob sent me a school exercise book with a red cover on which he had written my name. In 35 pages, in a fine, close hand, he had drawn up a kind of intellectual journal, more like an interior monologue than advice in the proper sense of

que conseils à proprement parler. C'est ainsi du moins que je le compris, et que je le comprends encore.

Je m'empressais de répondre – sans me laisser retarder par la préparation de mes examens – et je joignais à mes remerciements pour ce cadeau dont j'avais estimé tout le prix, l'expression naïve de mon admiration pour mon illustre aîné, sans aller toutefois jusqu'à le décorer du joli titre de 'Serviteur de l'Art'! Et plus naïvement encore je me permettais de discuter certains de ses aphorismes et de lui demander des précisions sur des points que je jugeais litigieux, voire erronnés. Enfin, dernière naïveté, je joignais à ma lettre deux poèmes que je soumettais à son jugement.

La réponse de Max Jacob ne se fit pas attendre: mes poèmes ne lui déplaisaient pas, mais il les trouvait dans l'ensemble trop littéraires, 'ce qui est un défaut, quand ce n'est pas une vertu.' Il préférait d'ailleurs me parler de 'questions générales', s'estimant 'très mauvais critique et plutôt à son aise en pédagogie esthétique'. Il prenait la peine de répondre à mon argumentation – ou à mes arguties – et de les réfuter sur deux grandes pages. Il m'expliquait l'importance du sentiment, des sentiments, l'importance d'allier les sentiments et les mots'. 'La poésie', me disait-il 'redeviendra humaine ou périra comme une inutilité.' Et il terminait malheureusement par cc post-scriptum, dont je ne compris pas sur le moment combien il était littéraire: 'Surtout ne soyez pas intimidé, dites moi 'merde' souvent. Je suis aussi débutant que vous, croyez-le.'

Et avec l'outrecuidance toute naturelle de la jeunesse, je le crus… Je lui écrivis donc une deuxième lettre pour défendre mon point de vue qui était alors celui du dandysme impassible et glacé, et qui s'opposait complètement au lyrisme chaleureux et humaniste que me prônait Max Jacob. Me croyant autorisé à parler en toute liberté, je le fis avec une intransigeance qui parut excessive à mon correspondant, et qui l'était sans doute. Sa réponse, sèche et brève, me remettait assez vertement

the word. At least that is how I understood it and how I understand it still.

I made haste to reply not letting my examination work delay me[1] – and added to my thanks for this gift, whose value I fully realized, the naive expression of my admiration for my illustrious elder, without, however, going so far as to confer on him the pretty title of 'Servant of Art'![2] And more naively still, I ventured to discuss certain of his aphorisms and to seek clarification on points I considered questionable, even wrong. Finally, ultimate naivety, I enclosed with my letter two poems submitted for his opinion.

Max Jacob's reply was not long in coming: he didn't dislike my poems, but he found them on the whole too literary, 'which is a fault, when it isn't a virtue'. Besides, he preferred to talk to me of 'general questions', considering himself 'a very bad critic and more at his ease as a teacher of aesthetics'. He took trouble to reply to my reasoning – or to my quibbling – and to refute it on two large pages. He explained to me the importance of feeling, of feelings, the importance of 'uniting feelings and words'. 'Poetry', he told me, 'will become human again or will perish as a thing of no use'. And unfortunately he ended with this postscript, whose literariness I did not at that moment realize: 'Above all, don't be intimidated, say 'Shit' to me often. I'm as much a beginner as you are, believe me'.

And with the quite natural presumption of youth I believed him... So I wrote him a second letter to defend my point of view, which was then that of impassible and icy dandyism, the very opposite of the warm and humanist lyricism that Max Jacob was preaching to me. Thinking myself authorised to speak in complete liberty I did so with an intransigence that appeared excessive to my correspondent, as no doubt it was. His reply, short and sharp, put me fairly roughly in my place and gave me to understand that our epistolary exchanges were at an end.

à ma place et me faisait comprendre que nos échanges épistolaires étaient terminés.

Max Jacob n'était pas du tout 'un fumeur sans tabac', c'était un vieux monsieur conscient de sa valeur, et il avait bien raison.

*

Je n'insisterai pas sur une dernière rencontre au cours de laquelle Max Jacob n'ajouta rien à ses 'conseils', mais parut manifester plus d'intérêt pour ma tournure que pour ma tournure d'esprit. Cela me déplut profondément et m'éloigna définitivement de cet être multiple, à la fois sérieux et bouffon, chaste et pervers, sincère et bluffeur, victime sans doute comme bien d'autres avant lui, comme Rimbaud peut-être, comme Jarry certainement, du personnage qu'il s'était lui-même imposé.

*

L'histoire du manuscrit, et de sa publication, mérite à son tour d'être contée. Dès le début, il avait suscité quelques convoitises. Marcel Béalu, que je m'honorais de fréquenter, le considérant non comme mon simple concitoyen mais comme le représentant, exilé en pays barbare, d'une sérénissime république des Lettres, ne fut pas le dernier à me le réclamer. Je le lui confiai volontiers et je lui permis, de bonne grâce, d'en prendre copie, ce que Max Jacob, je crois, avait omis de faire.

Là dessus, nos chemins bifurquèrent et chacun de nous s'en alla vers son destin. On connaît celui de Max Jacob. Le mien fut moins tragique; il se rapprocha davantage de celui d'Ezra Pound, enchaînés par d'autres bourreaux.

C'est ainsi qu'un jour, au travers des murs qui m'emprisonnaient, j'appris par hasard la parution du texte qui m'avait été adressé quelques années plus tôt et sur la première page duquel était écrit: 'Cahier appartenant à M. Jacques

Max Jacob was by no means 'a smoker without tobacco', he was an old gentleman aware of his worth, and he was quite right.

*

I will not lay stress on a last meeting in the course of which Max Jacob added nothing to his 'advice'[4] but appeared to show more interest in my figure than in my figures of speech. That deeply offended me and finally estranged me from this multiple being, at once serious and comical chaste and perverted, sincere and bluffing, no doubt the victim, as many others before him, as Rimbaud perhaps, as Jarry certainly, of the character he had thrust upon himself.

*

The story of the manuscript, and of its publication, deserves telling in its turn. From the outset a few people had coveted it. Marcel Béalu, whom I felt honoured to keep company with, considering him not as my simple fellow-citizen but as a representative, exiled in a barbarous land, of a most serene Republic of Letters, was not the last to demand it from me. I willingly entrusted it to him and with good grace permitted him to make a copy, which Max Jacob, I believe, had omitted to do!

Thereupon our ways parted and each of us went to meet his destiny. That of Max Jacob is well known. Mine was less tragic; it was closer to that of Ezra Pound, chained up by other tormentors.

So it was that one day, through the walls that imprisoned me, I learned by chance of the appearance of the text which had been addressed to me some years earlier and on the cover of which was written: 'Exercise book belonging to Mr. Jacques Evrard junior and drafted by Mr. Max Jacob of

Evrard fils et rédigé par M. Max Jacob de Saint Benoît-sur-Loire.' Personne n'avait cru bon de me demander mon avis, ni même de m'avertir de cette publication. Je ne m'étais jamais considéré comme le propriétaire de ces pages, mais personne ne pouvait nier que j'en fusse l'instigateur; Marcel Béalu moins que nul autre, puisque sans même chercher à savoir si j'étais vivant ou mort, libre ou reclus, il s'était senti obligé d'écrire quelques lignes à mon sujet.

Elles étaient suffisamment fielleuses pour qu'il ne se pressa pas de me les faire connaître lorsque je les lui réclamai. Et quand je les découvris enfin, je fus tristement surpris d'apprendre comment m'avaient vu ceux dont je m'étais cru l'ami. J'avais pensé qu'une sorte d''immunité poétique' nous protégerait, au moins les uns des autres. Il n'en était rien, l'époque était aux règlements de comptes.

*

Que reste-t-il, trente ans après, de ces pauvres querelles? Le centenaire de Max Jacob, seule pierre solide dans ce marécage.

Ces quelques explications, dont je remercie The Menard Press de m'avoir fourni l'occasion, ne valent guère que pour moi-même, et pour ce que je suis devenu: un 'jeune poète' qui a vieilli auprès de ses manuscrits. Je comprends aujourd'hui le dernier conseil de Max Jacob: 'Allez votre chemin et ayez confiance en vous-même. C'est la vieillesse qui a tort; clic a toujours tort. Travaillez! *Travaillez-VOUS*.'

Cela, je l'ai fait.

Jacques Evrard
Paris, Mai 1976

Saint-Benoît-sur-Loire'. No one had thought fit to ask my opinion or even to give me notice of this publication. I had never considered myself as the owner of these pages, but no one could deny that I was the instigator; Marcel Béalu least of all, since, without even trying to find out if I was alive or dead, free or in confinement, he had felt obliged to write a few lines about me.

They were sufficiently rancorous for him to be in no hurry to let me see them when I applied to him. And when at last I came upon them I was sadly surprised to learn how I had been regarded by those whose friend I believed I had been. I had thought that a kind of 'poetic immunity' would protect us, at least from each other. There was none, it was the period for the settling of accounts.

*

What remains, thirty years after, of these wretched feuds? The centenary of Max Jacob, only solid stone in this swamp.

These few explanations, made possible by an invitation for which I have to thank The Menard Press, are of little account for anyone but myself and what I have become: a 'young poet' who has grown old among his manuscripts. Today I understand Max Jacob's last advice: 'Go your way and trust in yourself. It's old age that is wrong; it is always wrong. Work! Work yourself *hard*!'

I have done that.

Jacques Evrard
Paris, May 1976

Translator's Notes

1. This alludes to Marcel Béalu's statement in his preface: 'Some weeks later the student, delayed no doubt by his examination work, thanked the author for this marvellous present by asking him for a definition of feeling. Max Jacob expected more enth-usiasm'.

2. Béalu quotes a letter from Max Jacob: 'He [Jacques Evrard] assures me of his admiration for a SERVANT OF ART (*sic*)'.

3. In the letter ridiculing the phrase 'Servant of Art' Max ends 'Everyone is wrong, I am a smoker without tobacco'.

4. According to Béalu, at that last meeting Max 'added a few pages to the exercise book'.

5. Max, quoted by Béalu, speaks of copies circulating.

The Authors

MAX JACOB

Max Jacob was born a Jew, in Quimper, Brittany in 1876. He made his home in Paris and was deeply involved in the literary, artistic and cultural revolution of his time. He is one of the most important and influential French writers and poets of the century and a great master of the prose poem, notably in *Le Cornet à dés*, 1917. Among his closest friends and colleagues in the early years were Picasso and Apollinaire. His published works also include novels and essays and many posthumous volumes of correspondence. In the later part of his life Jacob retired to the monastery at Saint-Benoît-sur-Loire: he had converted to Catholicism in 1915. He died, wearing the yellow star, at Drancy concentration camp, in 1944, but he retained his faith to the end, his last words being 'Je suis avec Dieu'.

EDMOND JABÈS

Edmond Jabès (Cairo, 1912–Paris, 1991) lived in Paris from 1957 until his death. He was awarded the Prix des Critiques in 1970. His major work was the seven-volume *Le livre des questions* published by Gallimard between 1963 and 1974. Rosmarie Waldrop's English translation (*The Book of Questions*) was published by Wesleyan University Press between 1976 and 1984. Subsequent translations of his work by Waldrop include *The Book of Shares* (University of Chicago Press, 1989), *The Book of Resemblances* (3 vols, Wesleyan, 1990–92), *The Little Book of Unsuspected Subversion* (Stanford University Press, 1996), and *From the Book to the Book: An Edmond Jabès Reader* (Wesleyan University Press, 1991).

JOHN ADLARD

John Adlard (1929–1993) taught in universities in Eastern and Western Europe and published a biography of Count Eric Stenbock, a study of folklore in Blake, a book on Apollinaire, a selection of Blake's poems, *The Debt to Pleasure*, an anthology of the work of John Wilmot, Earl of Rochester, and *The Fruit of That Forbidden Tree*, Restoration poems, songs and jests on the subject of sensual love.

www.ingramcontent.com/pod-product-compliance
Lightning Source LLC
Chambersburg PA
CBHW010042090426
42734CB00019B/3251